# APPLES OF GOLD

# Apples of Gold

By

Grace Noll Crowell

HARPER & BROTHERS, PUBLISHERS

*New York*

*A word fitly spoken*
*is like apples of gold in*
*pictures of silver.*

PROVERBS 25:11

¶ Credit is due the following publications for permission to reprint certain poems in this book:

*Augsburg Publishing House*
*Ave Maria*
*Capper's Farmer*
*Christian Advocate*
*Christian Herald*
*Christian Life & Times*
*Classmate*
*Dallas Morning News*
*David C. Cook Publishing Co.*
*General Mills*
*Good Housekeeping*
*Holland's Magazine*
*M. E. Church School*
*Nazarene Publications*
*National Historical Magazine*
*New York Sun*
*Oregonian*
*Pilgrim Press*
*Progressive Farmer*
*Quicksilver*
*Successful Farming*
*Unity*
*The Upper Room*
*War Cry*
*Washington Star*
*Westminster Magazine*
*Workers with Youth*

# CONTENTS

# APPLES OF GOLD

## Apples of Gold

OH, TO speak so fitly
That my words may be
Like bright golden apples
On a silver tree!

Oh, to write so wisely
That some hungering one
May reach and pluck that fruitage
Shining in the sun!

## Refrain

JOY and hope and peace,
   Sorrow, grief, and pain,
   All of life is sung
In this brief refrain;

All of life is lived
When these words are known;
When the heart has learned
Its lessons all alone.

Joy and hope and peace,
Sorrow, grief, and pain,
Life, I have heard you sing
Your brief sweet refrain.

Life, I have heard you tell
Simply all you know;
The music and the words—
I learned them long ago.

## Apples

ONCE in an old time garden of the world
A tree rose proudly upward from its root,
A tree so pleasant that a woman fell,
Tempted beyond resistance by its fruit.

"Stay me with flagons, comfort me with apples,"
A King in his dark hour cried for these,
And who in dreaming moments has not longed
For the golden apples of Hesperides?

And oh, that sudden scent upon the wind
Along old lonely roads and country lanes!
And the gleaming ruby and the golden lights
Among the grasses after autumn rains!

Yellow as harvest, russet as the hills,
The summer's bounty there for hands to glean;
Then suddenly the orchards are bereft
Save where the late-used reaching ladders lean.

## Accepted Praise

HE THANKS the Lord best who has given,
  Out of his own full-garnered store,
  A portion to others who have striven,
Yet failed to garner. Yea, the more
He shares, his gratitude lifts higher,
Like incense rising from the sod,
An acceptable, heart-warming fire
That takes its sure way up to God.

He thanks the Lord best who, rejoicing,
Refuses ever to be sad,
Whose prayer is filled with the glad voicing
Of the many blessings he has had.
He thanks his Lord best who, in serving,
Serves all mankind—His praises rise
Like a swift arrow, straight, unswerving,
Piercing the fabric of the skies.

## Keep Some Green Memory Alive

I SHALL keep some cool green memory in my
  heart
  To draw upon should days be bleak and cold.
I shall hold it like a cherished thing apart
To turn to now or when I shall be old:
Perhaps a sweeping meadow, brightly green,
Where grasses bend and the winds of heaven blow
Straight from the hand of God, as cool and clean
As anything the heart of man can know.

Or it may be this green remembered tree
That I shall turn to if the nights be long,
High on a hill, its cool boughs lifting free,
And from its tip, a wild bird's joyous song.
A weary city dweller to survive
Must keep some cool green memory alive.

## Wet Spring

IT WAS a wet spring, and the fields were lying
    idle,
  Waiting the plows and harrows, waiting the
    sun,
Yet the wind was high, and the steady rain kept
    falling,
The farmers were growing anxious with nothing
    done.
Some uttered the plaint that their families would
    be starving,
A bitter one cursed the ceaseless pouring rain,
But my father, who was a patient man, kept
    saying,
"It will all come right—the sun will shine again."

And now that his tired body long has rested
Deep in the earth he loved, his words still stand
True as the truth, and often when rain is falling
Overmuch on a troubled, waiting land,
And my heart is swept with the wind's incessant
    blowing,

And the day is dark as a turbulent storm-tossed
    night,
I can hear his words—and it comforts me—re-
    calling
That the sun did shine again, and it all came right.

## Kinswomen

I OWE a debt to those kinswomen of mine
Whose blood flows in my veins, exultant, free.
The things that make a commonplace day shine
Are good and gracious gifts they gave to me.
Mine were a simple folk, they loved the soil,
They loved the land and claimed it as their right.
They knew the blessedness of honest toil,
They loved their roof, their fire, their bed at night.

These, too, I cherish, and I often see
Some dear kinswoman of the long ago
Move out across the years to come to me
To talk of these good things we love and know:
Of households, husbands, children, and the near
Glad everydayness of all things held dear.

## Country Graveyard

HERE where the farmer folk, long dead, are
        lying,
        The weeds they ever fought close in at
        last,
Victorious now, with only a lone dove crying
In mourning for those whose simple life is past.
The moss-grown markers sag at their weary duty,
As tired as were the ones who fell on sleep.
Within this snarl of growth there is little beauty,
And nothing at all for the seeking heart to keep.

Even the once trim mounds can make no showing,
Leveled at last by time's relentless hand,
And yet the wind is sweet in its light-heart going,
And the sky is as blue as a gentian above the land,
And life is astir in the gnarled trees ceaselessly—
Even here there are signs of immortality.

## Summer Rain

NOW is the time the heart can love the rain:
The sturdy corn with laughter on its lips
Looks up to drink, and all the rippling
grain
Bears silver moisture on its bearded tips.
The clover is a mist of green and rose,
The wide alfalfa fields are silvered white
From the tossing wind, and from the rain that goes
Filled with its own peculiar silver light.

Now is the time the heart affords its rest,
Trusting a higher power to complete
The task at which the hands have done their best.
And now the summer rain comes cool and sweet:
A blessing on the thirsty soil and sod,
A benediction from the hand of God.

## Old Apple House in Autumn

SEEPING down from the cracks in the knotted
  ceiling,
 And lifting from the depths of the earthen
  floor,
An oddly released and subtle scent comes stealing
From the hoardings of many an autumn gone
  before.
And now afresh the Pippins, Baldwins and Russets
Heaped high in bushel baskets add their scent
To linger long in this ancient house long after
Their color is gone and their brief earth-life is
  spent.

Out of an orchard whose feet are ever wading
Ankle-deep in a glittering mountain stream
Have come the apples, crimson and green and
  golden,
As the bright fulfilment of some man's ancient
  dream
Of sturdy weighted trees whose abundant fruitage
Would gleam like lighted fires across the gloom
Of autumn days—waiting the inevitable hour
To be gathered close in the dusk of this mellow
  room.

## "Let Us Rest Awhile"

COME apart with me," the Master said,
"And let us rest awhile." O weary one,
How marvelous it is to be thus led:
To go apart with God's own precious Son,
And find his peace within that place of rest!
The secret of his calm serenity
Will be our own, and there we will be blest.
All this awaits, dear Hearts, for you and me.

Let us rest awhile there with the blessed Lord.
The burdens have been pressing overlong.
We need the wisdom of his spoken word,
We need to drop our cares and sing a song
There in the evening light: a song of praise
To him, the wise companion of our days.

## Fortified with Steel

"THE Lord thy God in the midst of thee is
      mighty,"
   The words shine out—and suddenly I feel
That I, who have been weak and far too fearful,
Am armored with bright steel.

"The Lord thy God in the midst of thee is mighty,"
I shall not fail whatever may betide.
His might, his strength, his power is in my being,
And he moves by my side.

"The Lord thy God in the midst of thee is mighty,"
O men, lay steadfast hold upon that truth.
It will be staying comfort for the aged,
And a forceful strength for youth.

O righteous nations, claim that proffered power.
It will not fail you in your crucial hour.

## God Is a Poet

GOD is a poet—more and more I find
The inner workings of his poet-mind.
I mark it as the seasons come and go:
Their rhythmic march, their unimpeded flow,
And in the sun's smooth swing, the rains that beat
Their music out on quick unstumbling feet.
The steady beating of the human heart
Beneath his hand is high poetic art.
The marvelous perfection of this flower
Within my hand denotes his lyric power.
And out across the meadows as I pass
I read his epic in the blowing grass.
God challenges each poet who would be
A candidate for immortality.

## Religious Freedom

ITS eternal price is eternal vigilance,
　And faith that sees the worth in any man;
　The knowledge that no good thing comes by
　　　chance,
But must be labored for. Since time began
The struggle has been bitter, hard and long
To keep a principle intact and whole,
As mankind sought to shield from hurt and wrong
The priceless freedom of the human soul.

Hardships were there, and rough the frontiers
　　　crossed,
And blood was spilled upon embattled sod,
That men's religious freedom not be lost,
As conscientiously they worshipped God.
O men, keep faith! Fight ever valiantly
That this great basic freedom be kept free!

# *War*

WAR! Oh, the torture, the hideous hor-
ror of it!
Man against man with a hate too
awful for naming.
The earth ashiver with shock and ever above it
The shriek and roar and scream, the scarlet flaming
Of death on the wind, and over and over the battle
Raging against the quiet stars, and under
The honeycombed ground, humanity huddled like
cattle
That are maddened by fright and the storm's wild
threatening thunder.

War! And the gentle Christ looking downward
and weeping
Above mankind as he once wept over a city,
Bewailing its awful sin, and still he is keeping
Watch above the earth that he died for. The pity
That men should betray One who loves us beyond
believing!
Ah, silent—yet louder than guns is the hurt
Christ's grieving.

## I Shall Go Out Alone

I SHALL go out alone
   Tonight beneath the stars,
   I shall forget the world
With its wars and rumors of wars;

I shall lift my face to the sky,
To its friendly fires and feel
The night winds reaching its hands
Into my heart to heal.

The darkness will soothe my eyes
That have looked too long at the light;
The clamor within my ears
Will cease in the soundless night;

And perhaps I shall find again
A thing I have lost for long:
Laughter upon my lips,
And a light-hearted song.

## After the Opera

THE curtain falls, and now a glare of light;
The throng of men and women move
apart,
Each carrying a dream into the night,
Each bearing aching beauty in the heart:
The imprint of those strange and lovely things,
The echo of the music's golden bars,
The sudden rifted clouds, the flashing wings,
As voices climbed to meet the glittering stars.

The arc lights prick the dark with fire flowers,
Harsh motors whir, yet men still walk in dreams,
Holding the memory of two jeweled hours,
Marking its brilliant shadows and its gleams.
The night has given something sought for long:
The old eternal passions set to song.

## The Seeker

I SAID in my grief, "I am hungering for the sea;
Surely its waves will soothe and comfort me;
Surely the turbulent sorrow it has known
Will be akin to this sorrow of my own."
So I went to the sea—I stood by its restless side,
I watched the endless ebb and flow of the tide—
I reached my hands, I lifted my voice to call,
Seeking its help, but it gave me no help at all.

Then I said, "I will turn to the mountains, they
        have stood
Through centuries of dark vicissitude,
And they will understand, and perhaps be stirred
To turn to me and utter the freeing word."
But the mountains stood unmoved, aloof, apart,
With never a word of comfort for my heart.

So belatedly I hastened for relief
To One who is acquainted with all grief
And knows all sorrow, and he turned to me
With understanding love and sympathy.

His eyes were kind—there was healing in his
    touch,
And I who had been needing help so much
Straightened with a quick and sure release,
Knowing at last I had found the source of peace.

## Our Daily Bread

AN ANCIENT rite, as old as life is old:
A woman baking bread above a flame.
Its value is far greater than pure gold;
It is ageless, timeless, and the simple name
Of "bread" is wholesome as the summer sun
That lit and warmed the fields that men might
eat.
It is as clean as are the winds that run
Their light-foot way across the waving wheat.

The loaf is only half a loaf unless
We share it, and unless we say
A grace above it, asking God to bless
The bread that he has given day by day.
O women, handle flour as you should!
It is a thing God-given, priceless, good.

## Suburban Street on a Summer Morning

THE shadows are black against the emerald
    velvet,
    And jewels gleam where sprinklers toss
    their spray,
While here and there a robin, gaily embroidered,
Slips through the glorious fabric of the day.

The terraced gardens are all ablaze with color:
The burning orange fire of a canna bed,
The larkspur's blue, and the marigold's hot
    flaming
Mingle with the salvia's smouldering red.

The houses, set well back, their doors flung open,
Are dappled black and gold by the arching trees;
A child runs out, a small dog barks his rapture,
A colored yard man toils upon his knees.

This lovely street with all its gracious beauty
Catches the heart, so clearly it is shown
How great the constant care, the intense loving
That men will give to homes they call their own.

## Silence

STRANGE how still these things
    Forever are:
    The sun, the earth as it swings,
A journeying star;
And the sod with its leafy joys
Makes no noise.

Strange that the heart can break
Without a sound,
And in its desolate wake
No wound be found.
And the deepest grief in the breast
Is the quietest.

The greatest love through the years
May be left untold.
How silent are the tears
Of the very old!
But death is the stillest thing
That time will bring.

## Secret Weapon

MORE powerful than any weapon known,
  Than bombs or tanks or guns or flame,
   far-thrown,
Is the secret weapon loosed upon the air
And designated by the brief word, Prayer.
A secret weapon, its component parts
Known only by the Maker of all hearts
That uses it with deft consummate skill
Of daily practice. Prayer that does not kill,
But succors lives of enemy and friend
For some high, glorious, eternal end;
Prayer that rises, and the answer speeds
Swifter than light to meet our crying needs;
Prayer loosed, and at its sudden swift release,
The anxious one has found a long-sought peace.

Oh, often battles have been won by these
Bright secret weapons—men upon their knees
Have brought strange victories to pass, have
  stayed
The onward tide of battle as they prayed.
God, God, today, may all men of all lands
Use oftener this weapon in their hands!

## Family Altars

IF EVERY home in every land had altars
   Where families worship daily and where
      prayer
Is lifted up, and God's dear Word held sacred,
With Christ a welcome guest beside them there,
The nations would not need to reassemble
In further parley over future peace,
For enmity and strife would be forgotten
And wars with their wild rumors all would cease.
The love of God is born at family altars,
Peace and goodwill to all mankind is part
Of any praying group's sincere devotion . . .
God, God, may every household take to heart
The old earth's deepest need, and rear their altars
Close by their own hearthside; and peace, long
      sought,
Will lave the earth because of mankind heeding
The vital lessons that the Master taught.

## The Promised Strength

ONE hour is not too long in time to wait
    For sorrow or for bitter pain to cease,
    If hope be there that someway soon or
       late
A healing hand will reach and bring release.
The weakest heart can bear that one brief hour
Courageously for courage's own sake,
If we but lean the while upon God's power,
And thus sustained, no troubled heart need break.

But look ahead to far-off months and years,
And the burden would become too great to bear.
O troubled one, look up and dry your tears,
God holds you in his everlasting care.
One step—and then another—breaks the days
To moments if the hours prove too long.
You will arrive, though devious be the ways,
And in God's promised strength you will be
    strong

### "He Sought to See Jesus"
### (Luke 19: 3-4)

ZACCHAEUS, I, too, would seek to see him;
I, too, would climb to some high place and
view
The Lord among the throngs that will not free
him,
For Zacchaeus, I, too, am small like you.

So little here among the throngs around him
In this bewildering day when men, to live,
Cry out in need and eagerly surround him
For the loaves and fishes that he has to give.

My need is great, O gentle Lord and Master!
I, too, would seek some spiritual high tree
And climb its leafy branches, fast and faster,
That there unhindered I may look on thee.

Behold me waiting now, dear Lord, I pray thee,
Call out to me and what I have is thine:
My table will be spread with bread to stay thee,
My door is open wide, come Lord, and dine!

## Self-Conquerors

TONIGHT I pray for all of those who
know
No surcease from some agonizing pain;
Who battle through the torture-dealing hours,
Counting them off as victors count their slain;
And counting them, if bravely they be met
With smiling face and clear unflinching eye,
As a triumphant victory, with God
Alone to know how deep the hurt may lie.

Theirs is an unapplauded fight, dear Lord,
Their march is not to music's ecstasy;
No buoyant strength is theirs, no zeal-fed fire—
Dismayed, distraught, yet uncomplainingly,
They fare them forth to face the bitter hours,
Knowing full well how rough will be the way.
Self-conquerors they go, these brave still ones:
It is for such as these, dear Lord, I pray

## Sinai

SOME evenings when the sun sets in wild
      splendor,
    I see Mount Sinai, through fire and smoke,
And I can hear a voice ring out as clearly
As it did the day when God Almighty spoke:

"If ye obey . . . Ye shall be a holy nation,
A peculiar treasure . . . All the earth is mine . . ."
His fingers move to write the ten commandments,
And on the stone the deeply etched words shine.

While I, at the foot of the mountain, one of
      many,
See silver flame shot through with amber light,
And I, too, tremble as the mountain trembles,
Shaken with awe and quivering with fright.

The voice of the trumpet sounds out loud and
      louder,
And his words: "Let not the people break the
      bounds

Lest they shall perish." Thank thee, God, for
    Moses,
Who has drawn a line upon the lower grounds.

In all of time there is no greater drama,
No grander setting than that mountain sky,
And no more vital words were ever written
Than those in the fire and smoke of Sinai.

## Sleep

THANK God for sleep! Without it none could rise
    Glad for the day, exultant with new strength;
Without it there would be but brassy skies
And hours dragging out their tortuous length.

But with it comes the freshening dew of night,
The quietness and peace of watching stars,
The first half-slumber where the little white,
Long-counted sheep leap over pasture bars.

Then rest so deep that weariness and pain
Are quite forgotten, and all sorrows fall
Away like full-blown petals in the rain.
Thank God for sleep—the greatest gift of all!

## Simple Art

THEY call her poor, the woman who lives
    there,
    Yet should they walk through her small
    house, a glance
Would prove that shabby rooms, loved much, may
    wear
A quiet elegance:

The elegance attained by simple art,
The art of making worn things take on light
Until each burnished surface is a part
Of one small house rubbed bright.

She stands her few plates in a glistening row;
Her furniture is scant, indeed, yet she
Sees to it that the old woods gleam and glow
Like polished ebony.

The silver shining of a pewter cup
Lit, by a hand that loves it, with a touch,
A vase with one flower in it, lifted up—
True, it is not much;

Yet someway, with that light upon her face,
No poverty can touch her, and to me
She, in her shabby house of ordered grace,
Moves with great dignity.

## Poem for an Unseen Guest

AS I would make my small rooms clean and
      sweet
    For some loved guest,
Burnishing and sweeping them that I
May give my best,
So Lord, today I fling the window wide
Within my breast

Ready for thee. I open my heart's door
To the clean air;
I let the wind and sunlight in, for no
Guest anywhere
Could be so welcome. Lord, here is thy room,
Thy bed, thy chair.

Abide with me—the best I have I give:
My bread and wine
I hasten now to share it all with thee,
O Guest Divine,
Be thou at home, move freely through my heart.
My house is thine.

## Young Girl in Spring

MY CALICO dress was a silvery sheath,
My sturdy shoes were as light as a
feather,
When I went out through the dappled woods,
A little girl in the glad May weather.
My basket of reeds was a thing of gold
With a glittering handle to swing and hold.

I was wild with joy at the first bluebell,
A-thrill with delight at a wild flower's capture,
While the sudden glimpse of a trillium bloom
Would stir my heart to exquisite rapture.
But oh, the heights of ecstasy when
I discovered the first wild cyclamen!

It was like a star that was shot from the sky
To fall at my feet like a radiant rocket.
I gathered it there—I gathered them all,
I filled my basket, my hat, my pocket:
A small happy vandal who did not know
That wild lovely things should be left where they
grow.

## A Windy Tree

A WINDY tree
    Is a beautiful sight,
    Filled with music
And gay with light.
And a wind-blown bird
In a wind-tossed tree
Is something joyous
And glad to see.
But the child at play
In the grass below
Is gladder than any
Thing I know!

## Youth Prays

WE ARE the young, Lord God, we need
Thy guidance;
We cannot judge the way that we
should go.
We find ourselves too often at the crossroads;
We pray Thee earnestly that we may know
And recognize at once the hidden dangers,
The lurking foes that surely lie in wait.
Help us to shun the wide road of destruction;
Help us to walk high-hearted, staunch and
straight,
Because we have the Comradeship of Jesus,
Who once was young as we are young today.
May He move out across the hills before us,
Our Leader and our Guide upon the way.
Thus would we reach the highest peaks, and
standing,
Facing the sun after the upward climb,
Envision there the task of world-wide service,
And thank Thee that we have the strength—the
time.

## Young Lincoln

ROUGH-HEWN walls and a sodded roof,
The latch string lax at the battened door,
The hearth flame climbing the chimney's
throat,
And a Youth stretched slim and long on the floor.
An open book in the firelight,
And flat on his stomach with earnest eyes
He scans the lines on the printed page
Seeking for truth that will make him wise.

A precious thing is that book to him,
Holding a knowledge beyond his ken.
How little he dreams in the firelight
That someday he, a leader of men,
Will utter words that the throngs will cheer:
Clear words that will ring while the old earth
stands—
A lad with his angular elbows bent,
And his dark head propped in his calloused hands.

## Letters

A SHEET of paper and a pen,
  And ink drawn from a bottled well;
  A heart, a hand, and lo, here is
A letter's fine material.

A white unbroken track that may
Become a lovely lasting thing:
A tracery in black to live
In some heart's fond remembering.

A thing of purpose and of strength,
A thing of beauty and of grace,
Reflecting in each mirrored line
The writer's heart and mind and face.

A fine immortalizing art,
The leisure art of ancient days,
Too apt to lose itself among
The snarl and tangle of our days.

## Old Autograph Album
### (Annabelle Endicott's 1810-1826)

THIS small book is a lovely thing,
As fragile as a butterfly's wing,
As delicate as a silver thread
Spun by a spider. Ah, the dead
Have left fine traceries to tell
They loved the young girl, Annabelle.

The ardent swains, with curleques
And flourishes and words profuse,
Insist that it will break their heart
If they are called upon to part
From Annabelle. And there still shines
Within these carefully penned lines
The clear undying flame of youth,
And something of the ageless truth
Of poetry. I turn each page,
Quite fearful lest through yellow age
They fall to ashes at my touch.
There is so much, so very much
The dead have left behind. Each page
Bespeaks a leisurely lived age,

With penmanship a practiced art.
I wish, I wish with all my heart
That modern pens behaved as well
As those addressing Annabelle!

## An Afternoon with Emily Dickinson

I SPENT this long sweet summer afternoon
With Emily beyond her lilac hedge.
New England is so beautiful in June,
And Emily delightful! The soft edge
Of her beruffled garments swept the grass
As swiftly down the garden walks she went,
Pausing a breath to watch a high lark pass,
A petal fall whose little life was spent.

Quick as the joy-mad lark her mind took hold
Of glistening fancies, and she set them free;
She shook out beauty for me to behold,
She opened up her shy wise heart to me.
Her voice was like a flute upon the air,
Her eyes were tender as an April dawn,
A sunbeam caught and quivered in her hair . . .
I reached to touch her hand, but she was gone.

## A Waxen Joan of Arc

A SACRIFICIAL candle
Upon a window sill
Stands tall and straight and lovely,
And very white and still,
Its slender yielding body
A waxen Joan of Arc,
A sheath that holds the spirit
Until a secret spark
Releases it; then upward
The lighted, living flame
Turns heavenward, the body
Returning whence it came.

A candle is so lovely
It touches me to see
Beauty long held captive,
Then suddenly set free,
Unbound, unleashed, unhindered,
Light-hearted, leaping, gay:
A vital thing set winging
Upon its upward way.

## Friendship

SO MANY friendships glow across the years:
    David and Jonathan, linked by hands of
       steel,
Sharing their strength, their laughter and their
    tears,
Knowing no grief the other did not feel.
There is no friendship that the world can know
Stronger than theirs of centuries ago.

Paul and Timothy—across the printed page
The two men go as one, within their hands
Were staffs of faith; and though another age
Laid hold of them, and far-off are the lands
Their firm feet trod, still through our memory
    wends
The lancelike figures of those timeless friends.

Happy is he who has a friend whose heart
Is tuned to his so that the memory
Of love will linger after they depart
Upon their journey to Eternity.
Happy are they so joined that men will know
Two walked the earth where one was wont to go.

## Destiny

THE sun and moon and stars do not stand
      still.
    Each takes its own peculiar certain way
Outward and upward, seeking to fulfill
Its destiny in its own separate way.
So shall I move forward toward the light
That draws me by the magic of its power
Forever upward, onward, night and day
To meet my own inevitable hour.

God is the center of that light—he stands
A magnet for the earth, the sea, the sky.
He holds the reins within his guiding hands;
The stars are safe with him, and so am I.
I, too, like they are part of the great plan
Outlined by him before the world began.

## Garden in the Sun

HERE is a woman's labor come to birth;
Here she is repaid for time and toil:
A blinding brilliance overflows the earth
And runs like light above the broken soil.
The heady phlox, the flaming marigolds,
The pungent gay nasturtiums in their bed
Toss in the wind—one single poppy holds
Color enough to dye the landscape red.
A woman's hands, a garden—a few seed,
And a wealth at last to meet the spirit's need.

## For the Guest Room

FRIEND, this is your room tonight:
   The bed, the table, chair and light
   Belong to you, not me.
Make use of them, I pray, and be
As much at home as if you were.
We trust that nothing shall occur
To mar your rest beneath this roof.
We give our love to you as proof
That we are glad to have you here.
So go to sleep without a fear,
And wake refreshed at morning light,
Rest sweetly then, Goodnight, Goodnight.

## A Sunny Room in Winter

SUMMER is captured here, the warmth and
     light
   Of fire and sun send out their golden glow;
A bright canary trills its keen delight
In liquid notes that leap and splash and flow;
And from a bulb-bowl piercing fronds arise,
A miniature green forest, pebble-strewn.
There is mid-summer in the light that lies
Across the rug this winter afternoon.

And such a sense of peace and deep content
Pervades this old worn room—such sunny cheer,
So many orderly and safe days are spent
Within its walls—such happiness is here;
So comfortable the chairs beside the hearth,
I love it more than any place on earth.

## Blind Singers

BESIDE the curb along the street,
Unmindful of the passing cars,
Two blind musicians stand and sing
Twanging their ancient worn guitars.

The windy day is April-sweet,
Even the city glimmers green;
The singers lift their sightless eyes
To sing of things they have not seen:
Of roses and of moonlit nights,
Of young love which they never knew,
With only the urchins down the street
To listen until their song is through.

But following me, the plaintive notes
Are sharp and keen—another spring
Swims in the lilac mist, and I
Am blinder than the ones who sing.

## Indian Farmer

I WATCHED an Indian at his primitive
    sowing:
He scattered the seed with a slowly out-thrust
    hand;
Across his harrowed acres he was going,
His shoulders shawled, his head bound with a
    band.
This first American had no need to hurry,
The land remained, and ever would be the same.
He had his faithful gods, why should he worry?
He had his squaw, and her oven's scarlet flame.

Should there be drought he would have no need
    to fear it,
He would climb the nearby hill and pray for rain;
Upon his adobe roof at night he would hear it,
And the rain god would walk through the rustling
    grain.
His corn would be tall for his growing sons to
    gather
When the autumn came with its smoke on hill and
    wood.
This stalwart native, no matter what the weather,
Will love his plot of ground, and find it good.

## Desert Sunset

ALL day long this desert land
    Has writhed beneath the furious heat
    Of molten brass poured on the land;
And now the night wind, cool and sweet,
Begins to stir the yucca's spines;
It shakes the ocatilla's tip,
And darkly where the low light shines,
The shadows of the desert slip.

And suddenly a dazzling light
Of mauve and green, that blurs my eyes,
Runs heralding the coming night.
Through pastel mists the mountains rise:
A radiance that has no name,
And he who waits has his reward,
Watching the scarlet tips of flame
That light the candles of the Lord.

## Desert Cactus

SUCH strange wild beauty in this desert
     place!
    Valiant and stalwart, yet a thing of grace,
Making its brave way toward the burning sky,
Armored with thorns, and yet with buds as shy
As any primrose as they blossom there,
Brilliant as jewels on the shimmering air,
Each spore an avid, heavenly reaching hand;
Its shadow, an oasis on the land.

"Useless," we say of this wild thing set loose,
Yet beauty is enough of an excuse
For any living thing; and God be praised
That in a barren land his hand has raised,
Cathedral-like, this cactus with its spires,
Its bloom, like many-colored window fires—
A challenge through the blinding, blistering heat
To any heart that would not know defeat.

## Sunset Fires

IF I could dip a brush in flame
  Or in pure molten gold, I might
  Set down a copy of the sun's
Clear painting on the sky tonight:
But I should have a wild-rose pink,
A nameless blue, a priceless jade,
A broader canvas, and a brush
Greater than man has ever made.
And I should have the skill of God,
His sure, unshaken hand, his heart.
Not having these I only can
Stand breathless—dumb before his art:
So drenched with color that my eyes
Are dazzled by it, and my hair
Is lit with golden dust where paint
Has dried and shattered on the air.

## Wild Life

I LIKE the quick bright movement of wild
      things:
  The unexpected flash of hidden wings,
The gold torch of a squirrel's tail flaming high
Against an arc of blue, bough-fretted sky;
A chipmunk's scamper through the autumn leaves,
The brown-striped pattern that his body weaves
Among the blowing grass; and down the slope
I like the action, the stiff-legged lope
Of startled deer; and from a mossy bog
The sudden splash of a green wide-spraddled
    frog;
The dart of iridescent dragonflies;
And oh, forever, wild wind from wilder skies
Sharp in dark branches where the leaves are
    thinned . . .
I think of all wild things I love the wind
More than anything that is set free—
There is something in it close akin to me!

## Marshland Dusk

DUSK on the wide low land—
The mirrored water showing
Silver among the reeds
Where the whispering night winds roam,
The rush of black-winged bats,
And dark on the after glowing
The circling whir of wings
Where the herons are coming home.

Careening over the bogs
The hurrying birds are falling
Into their rush-lined nests
After their headlong flight;
The croak of a diving frog,
And a killdee's plaintive calling,
And the flush of the twilight lost
In the deepening blue of night.

## Black Fruit

THE hackberry tree is black with fruit
Where the starlings seek their brittle loot
Of seed left by the last high wind;
And now that the rustling leaves have thinned
And the sprangled boughs stand still and stark,
Each seed is a clear-cut target mark
For the bullet bills of the plummeting birds;
And strange, what queer and chattering words
They employ at their accurate marksmanship
With a shattering seed at each bill's sharp tip;
And strange that a winter day can be
The fruiting time of a barren tree.

## Inscription on an Ancient Sun Dial

H ARK! "Yet a little while is the light with
        you,
    Walk while ye have the light," the Master
    said.
And deep in the fragrant green and mossy stillness
Of an old garden these carved words can be read,
Where an ancient sun dial marks the steady passing
Of the centuries gold sunny hours alone,
Giving wise counsel through its chosen motto
That runs like light along the lichened stone.

"Yet a little while," a gentle voice is speaking,
"Walk while ye have the light," Oh, wise is he
Who listens and who heeds that admonition
As a pilgrim journeying toward Eternity.
Come to that garden of tangled vines and flowers,
And learn from the dial to use life's sunny hours.

## Let Us Keep Christmas

WHATEVER else be lost among the
    years
    Let us keep Christmas still a shining
    thing;
Whatever doubts assail us, or what fears,
Let us hold close one day, remembering
Its poignant meaning for the hearts of men;
Let us get back our childlike faith again.

Wealth may have taken wings, yet still there are
Clear windowpanes to glow with candlelight;
There are boughs for garlands, and a tinsel star
To tip some little fir tree's lifted height.
There is no heart too heavy or too sad
But some small gift of love can make it glad.

And there are home-sweet rooms where laughter
    rings,
And we can sing the carols as of old.
Above the eastern hills a white star swings;
There is an ancient story to be told;
There are kind words and cheering words to say.
Let us be happy this glad Christ Child's day.

## The New Year

TIME is a gate in an ancient wall
That opens to let earth's pilgrims through
Onto a pristine meadowland,
Into a year that is strange and new.

No sign posts point out the road ahead,
No pathways lead where mankind has trod,
And none can see to the year's far length
Save the ever watchful, omnipotent God.

. . . . . . . . . . . .

Lord of the highroads of the world,
Lord of the years, oh, may we find
Waiting before us a better year
Than the darkened one we have left behind.

With its suspense, and the fear of war,
And the threatening thunders that did not cease.
Clear the skies for us, gracious Lord,
Give us the sun, and a world-wide peace.

## The Still, Far Places

HIGH are the cliffs at the edge of the sea
Where never a ship may go.
There only the wondrous wind-voiced
grass,
And the wild sea-blossoms grow,
And they wait, they wait in the hush of the days
When the sound of the sea is low.

Ah, long are the days in the yellow sun,
And long days under the clear blue sky,
With only the wind in the grass to go
Away where the big ships lie,
And only the flash of a gull's white wings,
And the sound of a sea bird's cry.

Unknown and undreamed is the far-off world,
Unknown is an upturned face,
And never an echo from steep to steep,
The sands bear no strange foot trace,
The still far places are God's alone,
The cliffs are his dwelling place.

## Thistles

WINTER was here but an hour ago,
And the spring—a moment gone,
The summer tarried a little while,
And then moved on.
Already the autumn must have come,
And swift as the wind will pass,
For I saw a thistle in bloom today
Deep in the wayside grass:
The first fringed thistle of the year!
And always the quick surprise,
And a sudden sadness clutching me
As before my eyes
The autumn marks its fleeting hour
With a wild, brief-blooming flower.

## Pigeons Above a City

I REMEMBER you, City—not your noise,
Your flashing signal lights, your signs that run
Like fire in quivering tubes; but I recall
With keen delight, three pigeons in the sun,
Leaving a cornice, lifting against the sky,
Quite undismayed by clamor and by smoke,
Or the siren of an ambulance that screamed
Below in the street's dark canyon. These birds
    spoke
A language all their own: Sheer radiant joy,
A rapture spelled with white wings as they rose,
The cleanness of far meadows, and the peace
That only untouched, unspoiled nature knows.
They etched their words upon my heart in white—
Those city aliens in their circling flight.

## A Voice

ONE night I heard a voice—Can I forget
    That living, laughing, sighing, sobbing
        thing?
Sometimes through waking hours I hear it yet,
Glinting, glancing, calling, whispering
To me of old time fountains in the sun,
And of old garden walks where roses cling.

I am not I, but rove enchanted lands
Through April twilights of far worlds and see
Jeweled Egyptian nights and moonlit sands,
The charm, the romance of old Italy—
I view it with high-lifted face, my heart
A-quiver with a strange wild ecstasy.

All this a voice! Through long forgotten years
One hour stands clear: the hour I heard it sing.
It is to me as when a harpist plays,
Glimpsing along each delicate taut string,
With my heart as the waiting harp, and I,
A poised, and breathless, watching, waiting thing.

## If I Could Know

I WOULD be richer by a thousand fold
   If I could know why certain poetry
   Has power to break my heart. If I were told
Why suddenly an ache should throb in me
As some sheer line of beauty, some turned phrase
Where the hands of a word-jeweler has set
His gems of living fire that through my days
Must be a thing my heart cannot forget.

Keat's nightingale, that strange, wild, deathless
      bird,
Will call to me forever down the years;
Through Shelley's odes, like some insistent word,
I shall hear the sea's voice heavy with its tears.
As Wordsworth "wandered lonely as a cloud,"
I, too, shall wander, and shall ever go
Lonely and hurt by beauty though the crowd
Be shrill about me. Why? I do not know.

## I Have the Faith

I HAVE the faith that Jesus
 Has the same power today
 To heal and bless and comfort
The pilgrims along earth's way,
As he had when he walked the highroads
Of earth and heard men cry
The poignant words that "Jesus
Of Nazareth passeth by."

I have the faith that his garments,
If touched, hold virtue still
That can straighten a crooked body,
And heal the maimed and ill.
I know that the broken-hearted,
The countless scores of them,
Have but to reach their hands out
And touch his garment's hem.
Lord, Lord, why should I waver
Through this strange night of grief?
I have faith—I know—O Master,
Help thou my unbelief!

## Followers

IN A far land and on an ancient day
 The great throngs followed him: the One who
  came
And said, "I am the Light," "I am the Way,"
And kindled in their hearts a leaping flame.
The tramping multitudes, the pressing throng,
That sought him for their own swift sure release
From shackling ills, or for some torturing wrong,
Sought avidly to find their soul's release.

Lord, Lord, today the throngs still reach to touch
Thy garment's hem across the lengthening years.
We have been hurt and troubled overmuch,
Look down and heal our ills, and calm our fears.
Behold the multitude that seek thee, Lord,
In church and field and lane of every land—
Speak peace once more, assure us through thy
 Word,
And bless us with thy out-stretched healing hand.

## "He That Keepeth Thee"

SO OFTEN in the dark hours of the night
It comforts me to know of one who stays
Close by my side, whose presence is a light
And a strength and solace through my nights and
    days.
And I am blest to know that as I sleep
He watches tenderly above me there,
And if I lie awake he stays to keep
Me comraded and safe within his care.

O Love that will not slumber when my need
Is great through wearing pain or bitter loss,
O Love compassionate enough to heed
My cry, and with the strength to lift the cross
That otherwise might crush me—Love divine,
I thank thee for this constant care of thine.

## In a Doctor's Reception Room

HERE are the Anxious gathered, here they
wait
The word, God grant, that may spell swift
release
From some dark hidden fear, and soon or late
The troubled ones may find a blessed peace.
The pain will lift, and they will walk again
In buoyant health among their fellowmen.

There may be those who face a graver test:
The steel-sharp knife beneath the surgeon's hands.
Their hearts are heavy weights within their breast,
Their courage daunted by strange new demands.
Strengthen that courage, Lord, and give them grace
To face the crucial hour they must face.

And if, dear Lord, the verdict holds no hope
For this brief life, Oh, be with them, I pray!
Go with them up the difficult steep slope
Which thy Son climbed that far-off April day.
Calmly and bravely may they turn and see
The waiting glories of Eternity.

## An Apple Falls

I HEARD an apple falling,
    And something in the sound
    Struck my heart as dully
As the apple struck the ground.
There was no wind to loosen
The ripe fruit from the tree;
No hand's impatient shaking
Had set that high bough free
Of its bright weight, and no one
Strode down the orchard grass—
Yet in that utter stillness
A strange thing came to pass:
One red globe among many
Was the first to fall—
I wonder why death chose it
From among them all?

## Walking Alone

I DO NOT need companionship while walking.
I would walk alone though the day be dark or
fair,
And never once would I feel the need of talking.
The raucous cries of the crows on the startled air
Is confusion enough for one who would be hearing
The voices of earth and sky and of blowing grass,
The cricket's chirp by the rail, and in the clearing
The sudden scamper of squirrels' feet as I pass.

How could I walk with a comrade and still listen
To the wind's clear singing high in the river reeds?
How could I catch the notes from throats that
glisten
Gold in the sun, or hear the jeweled seeds
Drop from their pods, and how could I be sensing
The corn's turned blades, the leaf print deep in
stone,
If I walked with another, volubly dispensing
Inanities? 'Twere better to walk alone!

## Autumn Flight

NOW are the wild geese going over,
  Clanking their chains on the windless sky,
  Over the cornfields, over the clover
Shouting their wild exuberant cry:
"Come with us, Come with us—Come." they are
    calling,
And I with no answer shaped in my mouth
Stand where the painted leaves are falling,
Watching them disappear in the South,

Disappear from my sight and hearing,
Going to who knows what far land
Straight as an arrow, and not fearing
The journey ahead . . . I lift my hand,
Bidding them stay their avid going
Across the wide and uncharted track,
Calling to them, and yet well knowing
That only the spring will bring them back.

## Poem for an Adopted Child

NOW. you are our own, our very Dear!
We have waited for you eagerly and long,
At last we are rewarded—you are here
Within our home and hearts where you belong.

You are adopted, truly, but be glad!
Walk proudly and serenely on the earth
Knowing that you are ours, as if we had
Been your own parents chosen at your birth.

Never forget it—ever be mindful of
That fact that we went out in search of you,
If you were our own flesh and blood, our love
Could not be greater for you, or more true.

God gave you to us—blest are we, indeed,
Before this wondrous favor, and we would
Pray earnestly to meet your every need,
And to rear you wisely, sanely, as we should.

## O Night of Wonder

O NIGHT of wonder and delight!
O night of glory and surprise!
With one road stretching clear and bright
Before our eager, dazzled eyes.

Drawn by the magnet of a star;
Drawn by an unseen power we take
A silver road that leads afar,
And follow it for Christ's dear sake.

O King of Kings, and Lord of Lords,
We fall before thy starlit throne.
Humble we are—there are no words
With which we fitly can make known

Our heart's elation and desire.
We search for words we cannot find—
The air is drenched with silver fire,
Too bright for eyes that are struck blind.

Accept our silence as high praise,
Our rapture, as a thing of worth.
We are stricken with the old amaze:
The strange sweet wonder of thy birth.

## Cherith

IT MUST have been so beautifully clear:
The little brook by which the Prophet dwelt.
Its gentle babble drew the ravens near
The sparkling brink, and when Elijah knelt
To cup the water for his thirst, there dropped
From golden beaks the bread that God had sent:
Metallic feathered birds that never stopped
Their ministry until the brook was spent.

I like to think of those brief hours of peace
For one man shut away the while with God:
A God who had the power to bid rains cease,
To stay the dew from drenching the parched sod.
A man content with neither script nor book
In God's companionship beside a brook.

## I Shall Be Remembering

I SHALL be remembering forever and forever
The old spring twilights along a country lane,
A tall row of maples, noisy with the chatter
Of blackbirds settling after a late rain.

I shall be remembering even up in Heaven
The red lights glowing across the fields I know;
I shall still be seeing a picket gate swinging
And through the dusk a lover, coming long
    ago.

Above the bright immortelles of the heavenly
    country
There will glimmer lilacs of an earthly spring,
Among the fields of asphodeles there will cling
    the fragrance
Of lilies-of-the-valley in my remembering.

And in some heavenly mansion—I shall not forget
    it—
A white house at evening, a curtain's blowing
    grace,

A firefly's blinking lantern, and in an open door-
  way
When I come home—the welcome on my mother's
  face.

*Blithe Spirit*
(For J.W.W.)

NOW with the difficult roadways in the past,
    And the tiring, rugged hills all climbed
        at last,
There must be other hills, but hills so bright
And gentle to climb there in the heavenly light
That your blithe spirit surely will take wing
Jubilantly, and the songs you sing
Will echo back as crystal-clear as glass.
Your feet, swift as the wind, will cross the grass,
And the poems you have longed to pen will well
Like some unsealed bright fountain, there to tell
Of beauty that you ever sought for here.
O lovely one, O infinitely dear,
All unencumbered now, and free as air—
Surely all Heaven is brighter with you there.

## If You Reach Heaven First

IF YOU reach Heaven first—please wait for me.
   I do not think that it could be for long.
   I know how vast must be Eternity,
And I might lose my way among the throng,
And I might miss you—I might fall behind,
Though I would go on eager hurrying feet,
Seeking for you, and yet fail to find
You down some golden lane or glittering street.

We have been together for so long on earth,
God has been good to spare us year by year
To share the same snug roof, the same warm
      hearth—
I have depended so upon you here,
That Heaven with all its glory would not be
Complete at all if you were not with me.

*Set in Intertype Garamond*
*Format by A. W. Rushmore*
*Manufactured by The Haddon Craftsmen*
*Published by* HARPER & BROTHERS
*New York*